C. Reichert.

A *Dog* BLESSING

LAUGHING ELEPHANT BOOKS   MMII

LAUGHING ELEPHANT BOOKS
3645 INTERLAKE AVE N.   SEATTLE WASHINGTON 98103
WWW.LAUGHINGELEPHANT.COM

Dogs are our oldest friends, our best companions.
We offer here a blessing for them,
and for those who share their lives.
We are ever grateful for their presence.

Big or small, they are our guardians.

3

They take a childlike delight in
everyday things and events,

finding life always new and exciting.

Dogs love laughter, play and good times,

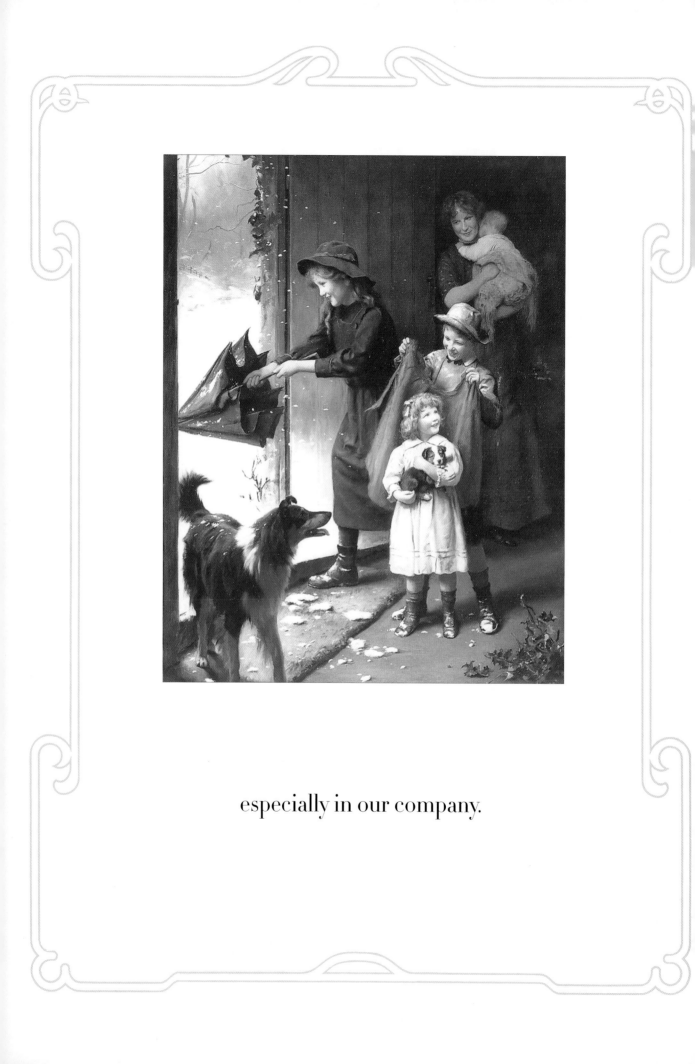

especially in our company.

They are sensitive to our moods,

sorrowing if we sorrow,
echoing our joys.

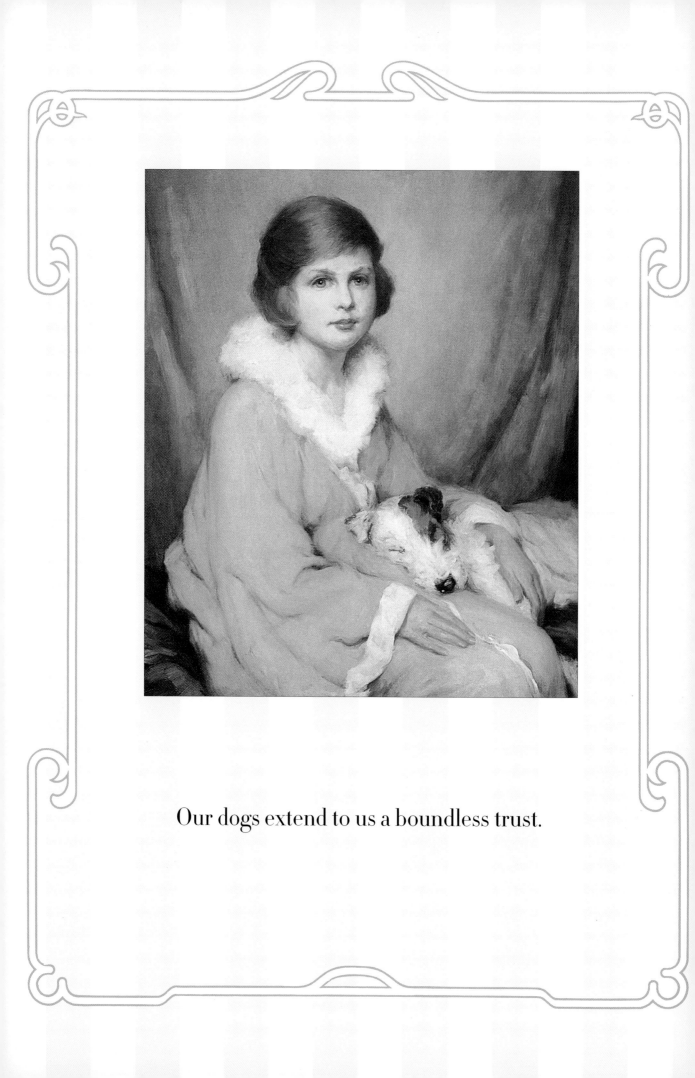

Our dogs extend to us a boundless trust.

They prefer our company over all others.

Dogs have an innate dignity,

and love to help us in any way.

Dogs are a great source of loving laughter.

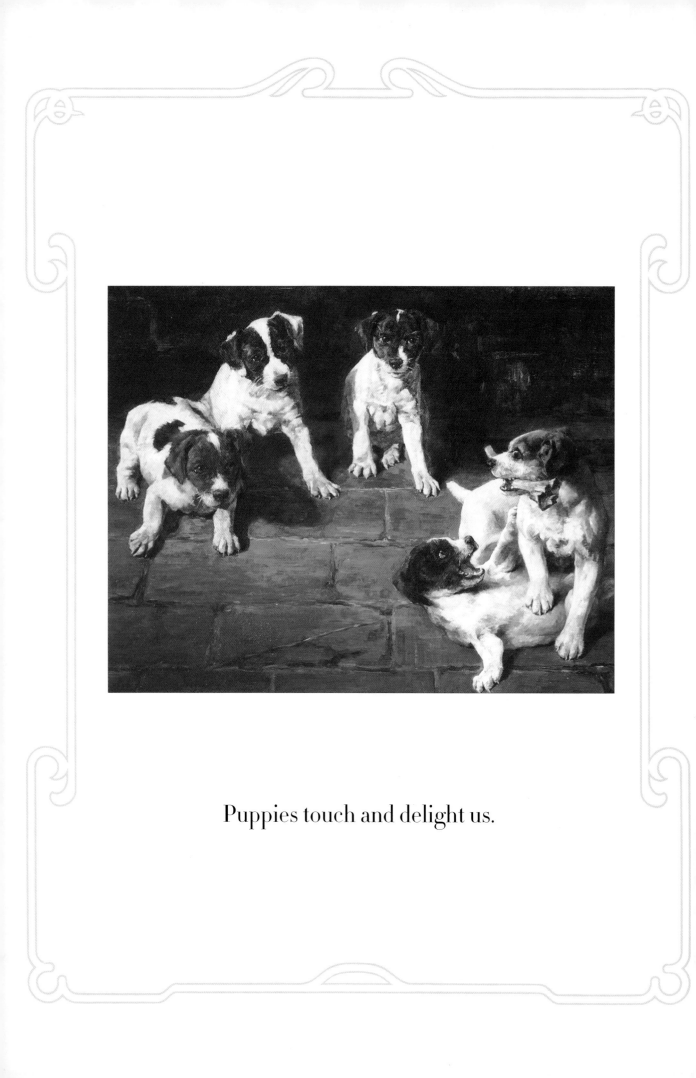

Puppies touch and delight us.

We are pleased to have the focused attention
of our dogs,

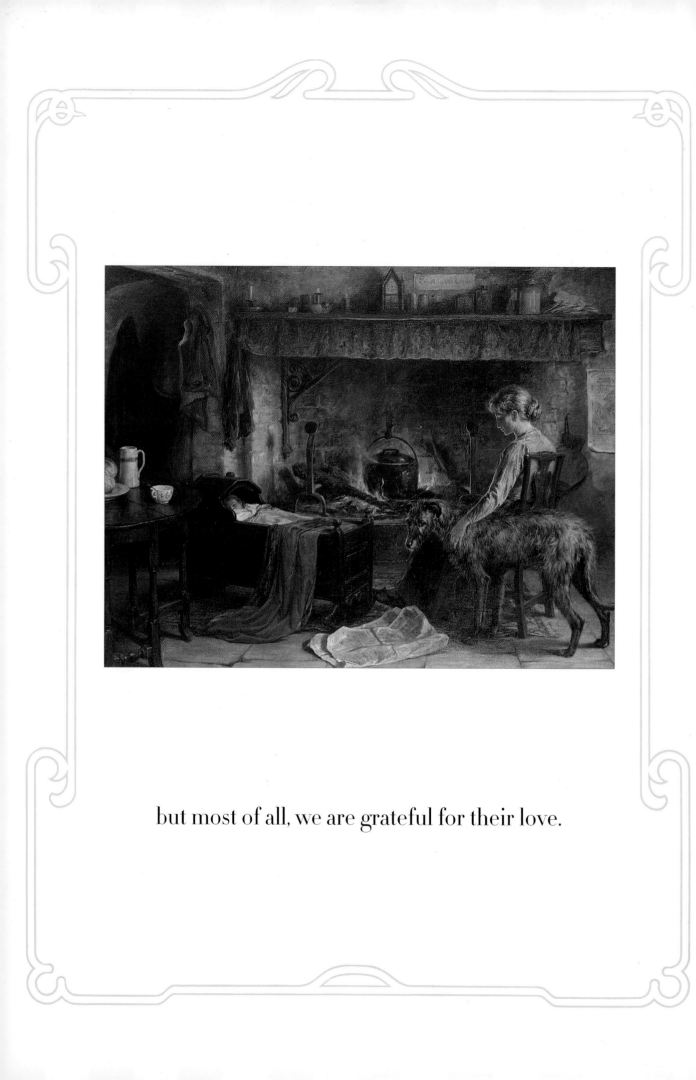

but most of all, we are grateful for their love.

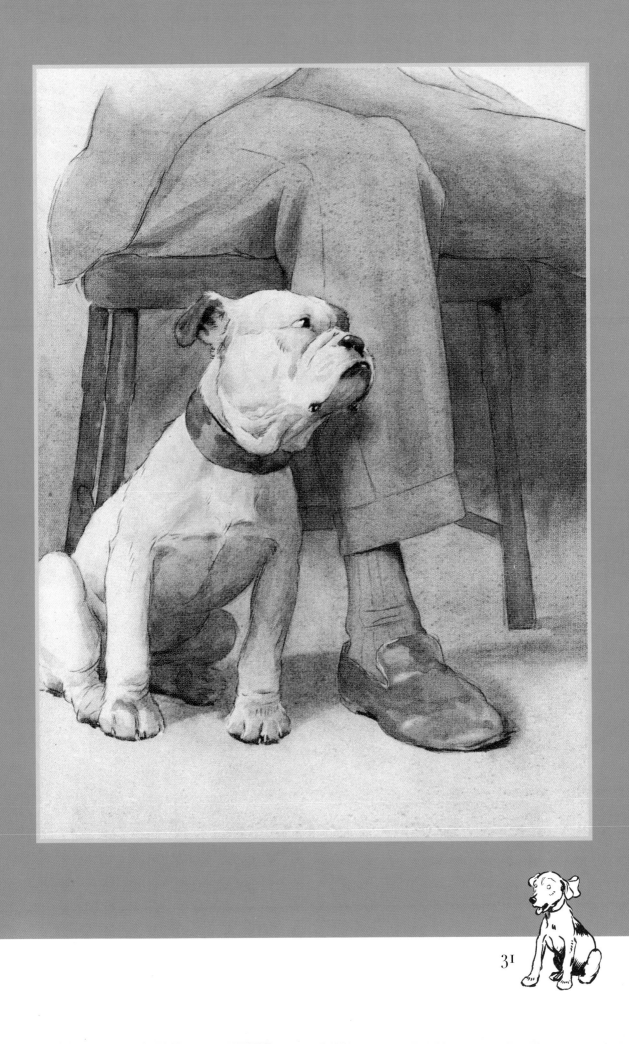

Picture Credits

Cover	Cecil Aldin. From *Dogs of Character,* 1927.
Endpapers	Clara Tice. From *ABC Dogs,* 1940.
Half-Title	Josephine Crumrine. "Smokey," ca. 1940.
Frontis	Carl Reichert. "Studies of Dogs," n.d.
Title Page	Lilian Cheviot. "Royal, a tricolour working Springer Spaniel," n.d.
VIII	Anonymous Postcard, c. 1913.
IX	Trübner. "Dog and Sausage," 1878.
Page 1.	Maud Earl. From *Memories,* 1914.
Page 2	Eugen Felix. "Guarding the Baby," n.d.
Page 3	Anonymous illustration, n.d.
Page 4	Arthur Wardle. "Terriers on the Scent," n.c.
Page 5	Arthur Wardle. "Cocker Spaniels," n.d.
Page 6	Florence E. Seyfarth. From *Fall is Here,* 1948.
Page 7	R.S. Moseley. "Chow-Chow in a Forest," 1897.
Page 8	Louis Agassiz Fuertes. From *The Book of Dogs,* 1919.
Page 9	Arthur J. Elsley. "You Dursn't," 1905.
Page 10	Arthur J. Elsley. "Home At Last," 1918.
Page 11	Annie Benson Müller. "A Country Gentleman," 1937.
Page 12	Anders Zorn. "Clarence Barker," 1885.
Page 13	Will Houghton. Poster design, n.d.
Page 14	Arthur J. Elsley. "The Tea Party, 1909.
Page 15	Briton Rivière. "Sympathy," 1877.
Page 16	Percy Harland Fisher. "Her Favorite Pet," n.d.
Page 17	Anonymous illustration, n.d.
Page 18	Unknown. Magazine cover, 1937.

Picture Credits

Colophon

Designed at Blue Lantern Studio
by Sacheverell Darling & Mike Harrison

Typeset in Didot & Bickham Script